GIAN CARLO
MENOTTI

FANTASIA
for cello and orchestra

(reduction for cello & piano)

ED 4062
first printing: July 2001

ISBN 0-634-00667-3

G. SCHIRMER, Inc.

DISTRIBUTED BY

HAL•LEONARD®
CORPORATION

7777 W. BLUEMOUND RD. P.O. BOX 13819 MILWAUKEE, WI 53213

The Fantasia *was first performed*
January 16, 1976
by Laurence Lesser, cello, with the RAI Orchestra,
Turin, Italy.

The solo part
has been edited by Carter Brey.

INSTRUMENTATION

Solo Cello

Piccolo
2 Flutes
2 Oboes
English Horn
2 Clarinets in B♭
Bass Clarinet
2 Bassoons

4 Horns in F
2 Trumpets in C
3 Trombones
Tuba

Timpani
Percussion (2 players):
    Xylophone, Triangle, Tambourine,
    Cymbals, Snare Drum, Bass Drum

Harp

Strings

duration: ca. 20 minutes

FANTASIA
for cello and orchestra

Gian Carlo Menotti
(1975)
edited by Carter Brey

poco rall.

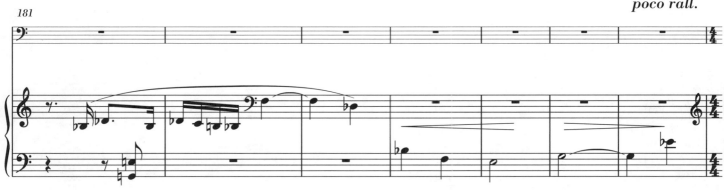

Ⓚ

a tempo

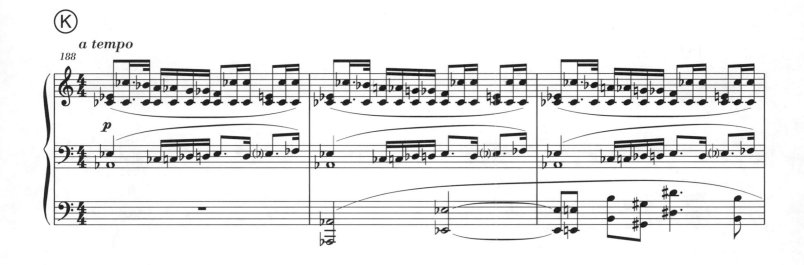

un poco più movimentato e rubato

poco rit. *al tempo di prima*